AF605154

AUSTRALIA

First published in 2025 by New Holland Publishers
Sydney, Australia.
newhollandpublishers.com

 A record of this book is held at the National Library of Australia.

ISBN: 9781760797843

Managing Director: Fiona Schultz
General Manager/Publisher: Olga Dementiev
Designer: Andrew Davies
Production Director: Arlene Gippert
Printed in China

AUSTRALIA

AMP

Marriott

PARK

02

ART GALLERY OF NEW SOUTH WALES
GIOTTO

useum of
Contemporary
Art

DOYLES
Doyles
ESTABLISHED
YEARS

15
NO STOPPING
OR DRIFTING

#TamworthNSW

THE
BIG
GOLDEN GUITAR
TOURIST CENTRE

THE BIG
BANANA
COFFS HARBOUR

MUSEUM
QUEENSLAND
MUSEUM

EXIT

BUNDABERG
ESTD RUM 1888
ORIGINAL
CRAFTED IN AUSTRALIA
EST 1888
UNDERPROOF RUM
700mL 37% ALC/VOL
BUNDABERG DISTILLERY
WHITTRED ST.QLD

THE AUSTRALIAN

CKMAN'S HALL OF FAME
AND OUTBACK HERITAGE CENTRE

CITY OF CANBERRA
QANTAS

QANTAS
VH-XBA
OVERSEAS AIRLINE

RioTinto
LAVAN LAVAN

V R
1855

G
H
E
F
No 1 DIVISION

German Village Shop
German Village Shop
50

Christmas
Shop & Gifts
German
Cuckoo Clocks

ANDAMOOKA
OPAL HOTEL
BARGAINS
ANDAMOOKA
OPAL HOTEL

ANDAMOOKA
OPAL
HOTEL MOTEL
ANDAMOOKA
OPAL HOTEL
the last

acmi

Luna Park

C42

AUSTRALIA

- Australia is the only country that can also be considered a **continent**.
- Australia is the **6th** largest country in the world!
- The official language in Australia is English.
- The population is over **26 million** people.
- Australians are known as Aussies and have their own unique language called the **Aussie Slang**.
- Australia is home to the oldest living fossils on earth, and the **Great Barrier Reef** is the largest coral reef system in the world.

- The capital of Australia is **Canberra** where the national government is located.
- There are over **10,000 beaches** in Australia.
- Over **85%** of Australia's population live on the coast.
- Australia has numerous **beaches** which may have some of the whitest sand in the world!
- Australia has some of the most **unique wildlife** that can only be found in Australia.
- The **Kangaroo** is Australia's national animal and **Emu** the national bird.
- While Australia has a huge amount of seafood, the roast lamb has been declared Australia's national dish.
- Australia's highest mountain is **Mt Kosciuszko**, standing a mere 2,228 metres high.